Esther's

Soul

Trupti Desai

Published by: Roaring Lambs Publishing,
www.RoaringLambs.org
Published in the United States of America.

Acknowledgments

I dedicate this book to my three children who are wonderful gifts and blessings from God.

To my incredible mother, a woman of great faith, who through her struggles, taught me to never give up. I am grateful for her humble and loving heart.

I am indebted to the Holy Spirit for the inspirational, anointed words that gave life to *Esther's Soul*.

To my beloved Jesus who redeemed me and transformed my life.

I am in awe of my Father in Heaven, who never gave up on me and has rescued me countless times. I am grateful for all His blessings and humbled by His love, mercy, and divine guidance.

Contents

My Testimony

What is that empty feeling?
A burning in my soul
A desperate need to fill this void
This deep desire to connect
There must be something more.

Somewhere deep within me from a very young age, I knew there was something more. More than I could see in the visible world.

I was born into a poor, devout Hindu family in a small town in Zimbabwe, Africa. As it was during apartheid and the forced separation of the races, I was set apart from birth with my mother delivering me in the non-white wing of the hospital.

My first home was the unused rooms of a dusty storefront in the African bush next to the roadway. Nearby was an old well where my mother would get water. There were no other buildings near us. We were isolated and surrounded by trees and tall, brown savanna grass.

I would grow up learning the Hindu ways of worship and blindly following what I was taught. I never questioned my mother's teachings that were based on centuries-old Hindu doctrines.

I would sit daily in front of the idols with

rosary beads, chanting the Gayatri mantra, sometimes 108 times a day. My mother would teach me that God was to be revered, and I knew at a very young age that He was powerful and to be respectfully feared.

Indoctrinated with the belief that the Hindu idols would deliver me from evil and grant me success in every endeavor of my life, my Hindu worship became a series of habits and rituals that I did not fully understand but followed for decades.

However, even as a child I innately understood that there was something more I was seeking.

The first moment, I realized there was a God who spoke to me, was when I was four years old. My father had tried to kill himself. I heard the commotion, and as my mother frantically called the ambulance, I ran to my father to see blood and panic everywhere.

As they wheeled my father away, I ran after him calling to him. "Papa, Papa don't leave me!" I watched the ambulance speed away.

Sitting outside alone on the steps, rocking to and fro and numb with pain, I suddenly felt something come over me. It was like a comforting warm blanket, and I will never forget the voice I heard. "It's okay. It's okay."

Somehow, I knew that this secret God who was talking to me felt loving and kind, unlike the cold, inanimate Hindu idols that did not communicate with me.

My father thankfully survived and would come back home, still a troubled soul.

It was many years later when I heard the voice of God again, speaking into my soul and this time directing my steps. I was twelve years old, and with great clarity, my secret God told me that I was and leave my hometown and go into the world.

After being a below-average and troubled child, I would suddenly excel in many areas of my life. I was determined to get to the only university in Zimbabwe at that time. The competition was fierce, but so was I. It was my one-way ticket to escape my country and succeed in the world. I became a hardworking, intellectual leader with a burning desire to survive and win, despite many emotional and financial obstacles.

During my teenage years, I felt a stronger connection to the God that had called out to me when I was four. This other God. This secret God. The God that I did not tell anyone about. The God that I could call to after I had been viciously bullied or who had saved me from sexual attack. The times

I ran away from my father's beatings and sat alone in the dark. He was my God. My Friend. He was always there no matter what. He gave me hope and comfort when I felt so alone.

The relationship would grow, and I would develop an internal compass, instinct to hear, follow and, connect with my secret God often.

I would converse with Him about my life.

I questioned Him, thanked Him, and there were even times I yelled at Him. The times I would hear His voice were mostly during critical life decisions, and I would obey. It was His comforting presence that I desperately needed during the dark lonely times. I just needed to know He was there.

During my teenage years I also asked many questions and had a desire to discover who I was and, the purpose of my existence. I had a powerful need within me to seek meaning, truth, and a destiny. My God had whispered in my ear that He had called me to do something, and a burning desire was created deep in my soul to seek this truth, this calling. Until I fòund this "truth", I would not find peace.

I began to read voraciously and study the occult. I believed that astrology would surely reveal who I really was and my purpose. I explored palmistry, and my spiritual powers increased. At the age of nineteen I became well known in the community. People would form long lines to visit me at Indian weddings and events where I would read their palms for free, even late into the night.

During my twenties, I constantly questioned God and would spend a lot of time alone with Him. Why was I different? Why did I not fit in?

I could not connect fully to my Indian heritage and felt apart from my people. Who was I? The desire to please my God and discover my destiny was overwhelming.

There were times I would fall on my knees and yell at God with tears streaming down my face, "What do You want from me!?"

It would take decades till my soul finally found peace.

I accomplished my goal to get to the University of Zimbabwe and got a Bachelor of Science Degree. I began to look to science as my authority. I loved the intellectual challenge, research, logic, and apparent truth that science brings.

However, studying science, palm reading, and astrology were still not enough to satisfy my soul. Over decades, I would seek psychics, tarot readers, and yes, even advice from a witch doctor in my home country.

In trying to fill that empty part of my soul, I would turn to self-help courses and books, Oprah, Eckhardt Tolle, Scientology, crystals, intellectuals, and anyone who appeared to know the deeper things of life.

With child-like faith I foolishly believed that if there was some truth in what I heard from these various sources it was to be believed.

I have learned the hard way how dangerous it is to fall for a semblance of truth, to only find out it was surrounded by a plethora of lies, and I would pay a heavy price.

However, it never occurred me, during decades of searching, to ask my secret God to give me an answer to that empty part of my soul. The answer to the elusive truth I relentlessly sought after.

Little did I realize that a day would come that God himself would reveal a truth so complete, absolute, and divine that would finally give me the answer to the "something" I so desperately needed to know.

As God had instructed me when I was twelve years old, I left my country to work in London. I also had incredible adventures traveling to different countries and places.

During my travels I encountered joy and pain. I lived in absolute awe of God's majestic landscapes, and I wept when I saw poverty and pain in some of the poorest parts of the world. "Why God why?"

During my travels I would meet my future husband and move to America.

Over the decades, I never stopped seeking my Lord. He was always my go-to when I was in pain, as I would tell myself the words repeatedly, "It's okay. It's okay."

He always gave me a sense of comfort, hope, and the strength to carry on, as I would fall on my knees sobbing in pain after yet another traumatic experience. My God was the one who gave me the resilience to survive and pick myself up for the next battle. I instinctively knew that I was in a war.

I was constantly on the battlefield, fending off first the trauma of my father, then bullying, physical attack, debilitating sickness, near-death experiences, financial theft, rejection, emotional abuse, and mental torment.

There was a continuous assault on my mind, body, soul, identity, and self-worth. However, I was determined to survive, and I knew the one place to live and fight another day was not something that the world would give, but my secret God. He is and will always be my desperate addiction.

In May 2015, I would come across a Christian Lyft driver who was a converted Muslim man from Iran. He had studied the Bible and was well conversed in the ways of God's word. For some reason, I trusted him and requested he take me to the airport many times over the next months, as I had to travel for work.

I believe it was the third trip to the airport when he boldly told me that I was missing Jesus from my life, as he knew I was not a follower of Christ. I mocked him and Jesus. I point-blank let him know that there was no way that there was only one way to God. How could he say that Jesus was the only way to God?

I questioned him. "Do you know that I have been connected to God all my life?" Do you know how many false Christians I have come across and hurt me? Do you know that my mom is a wonderful humble woman who prays daily to her Hindu Gods?"

I resisted. He persisted.

A few months later I found myself once more on my knees pleading and crying to my secret God. I had lost my job. It was the third job I had lost in only two years. At this point in my life, I was a divorced mom with three young children, having left a difficult, thirteen-year marriage.

I had worked hard and had transitioned my career over the decades from a Science teacher to an IT consultant to a Vice President of Data Analytics. Every job I lost was due to a political attack, over which I had no control. It was interesting, though that with each job loss I would get a salary increase and be promoted. However, at this point I was exhausted and despondent. I went to the one place where I knew I would find comfort and strength to get through the dark nights. My secret God.

This time was different. In fervent desperation I asked God, "How is this fair? I have loved You all my life. I have been faithful. I have prayed. I have feared You. I have chased You my whole life and stayed close to You. You are my God. I cannot live without You. But what do You want from me? What am I supposed do to stop this vicious cycle of a lifetime of constant attacks? Is it my fault?"

I earnestly thanked Him for giving me the strength to fight many attacks and battles but was at the point of utter surrender. "I give up, my God! I cannot go on with this torment in my life and soul."

I began to ask myself these questions. Was it true then? Was Jesus the way to peace and rest? Would He remove the constant torment from my soul? Was Jesus missing from my life?

I knelt in front of my God, crying in pain, and asked Him to tell me the truth. I boldly demanded of my secret God to give me an answer. "Tell me, my God". Tell me the truth. It is only You I trust."

I began to embark on a search for the absolute truth. All my experiences, self-help courses, and knowledge collected over decades had not been enough to quieten my soul. Greatly determined to understand this elusive Jesus, I began to voraciously study the Bible. The logical, fact-driven part of my mind was in unbelievable awe of the proven historical accounts and thousands of prophecies that had been fulfilled with incredible accuracy and precision.

About three months later after I had sat in my room pleading with God to tell me the truth about Jesus, I met this lovely Christian lady called Jan. We conversed and I let her know about my quest to find the truth about Jesus. After completing our conversation, she gave me a book called "More Than a Carpenter" by Josh and Sean McDowell. She also told me that the most important thing was to have relationship with Jesus.

It was the word "relationship" that began to intrigue me even more about by Jesus. After all, I had a lifelong, connected relationship with my God. Also, it made no sense to me at all that I would be saved by just saying the prayer of salvation without meaning and believing it from my heart.

"More Than a Carpenter" was a fascinating read. The specific texts that captured my mind were the myriad of details that had to materialize to bring forth the birth and death of Jesus. The precise lineage, address place, time, manner of birth, and manner of death identified God's son, the Savior of the world, hundreds of years prior to His birth. There was no doubt in my mind after reading the book that Jesus was real and had come to earth thousands of years ago.

I also started watching a Bible series and it came to the point of Jesus's crucifixion. I remember that night vividly. It was almost as if I was at the foot of the cross with Jesus. My heart felt such love, compassion, and pain and I cried uncontrollably as I watched Him go through such excruciating torture. It struck me that there was no one else in any religion that had willingly died for the truth. When He said, "Father forgive them for they do not know what they do," it was in that moment that I truly understood the power of unconditional love and that He had died for all of humanity.

Six months had now passed since I had asked my secret God to tell me the truth about Jesus when I got a call from the Iranian Lyft Driver to attend a Bible study. I had never been to a Bible study before and had a lot going on that day. However, my inner compass was directing me to attend.

I also could not get out of my mind that I had not heard from God or felt His presence for a while. There was intense burning inside of me to hear from Him. I was getting desperate and needed to know the answer to the questions that had burned in my soul over the last six months. Would Jesus calm my tormented soul? Was Jesus ultimately the only way to meet my secret God? Even though I had discovered so many truths and facts about Jesus, it was only my God, who I trusted, regardless of how much knowledge I had collected.

However, I did wonder if God was orchestrating many of the encounters, I was exposed to over the prior six months. Somehow, I was always meeting the right people at the right time to give me a message, a book, or a word about Jesus to further my journey.

I walked into the door and noticed many crosses on the walls and a peaceful, almost holy energy.

The Bible study was interesting, and I enjoyed the worship music. An hour later we circled in a small group to pray.

It came to my turn to pray and crying in desperation I looked up to God begging Him to tell me the truth. "Tell me!"

At that very moment, a powerful force pushed me back, and I fell onto the couch behind me.

I was filled with a new life force that had the power to hold me down and I started to rapidly utter a new language. During the commotion, I sensed something behind me. I was compelled to turn my head upward and there was Jesus! He appeared tall with brown hair and had a purple robe and a crown. His deep-set eyes burned like sapphires, and it was a bold confirmation from my secret God. My God had directly answered my petition! He showed me without a doubt that indeed Jesus was the Way, the Truth, and the Life, and He also was presented as a King.

Jesus answered, "I am the way and the truth and the life. No one comes to the Father except through me."

John 14.6 (ESV)

The relentless search to find solace for the empty part of my soul would lead me to a truth that I did not expect. I would come to understand a few years later that He had chased after me. He left the ninety-nine, to find His lost sheep, not willing to leave me behind. I am so intensely grateful that He never gave up on me and that I never gave up on Him.

I never truly understood a father's love as I mostly feared mine. I have always loved my earth father dearly and know he had his own demons to contend with, and that he always loved me in his own way too. I now call my God, my Father. When we converse in times of stillness and prayer, in His gentle way, He ministers to my heart so that I can heal. I have learned to receive His deep love and know that I am His beloved daughter.

I have been blessed to see Jesus a few more times since I was saved. It is very humbling and overwhelming. Time appears to stand still, and each moment is significant. He always looks the same physically, but I wonder about the color of His eyes as they seem to vary. I believe I had a chance to see His spiritual eyes when I got saved. I felt like I was falling into His sapphire eyes deeper than the ocean and more beautiful than anything I have ever seen.

It would take forty years for me to be saved by Jesus after my first encounter with God at the age of four. It was a miraculous encounter, and my life has transformed since. I am now on a new journey with my God, Jesus, and the Holy Spirit. Blessings and favor abound. Two weeks after I got saved, I received a call out of the blue for an amazing job and have been with the same company, which I love, ever since.

I am very blessed to have Jesus in my life, and the journey continues to be transformational, fruitful, loving, and miraculous. Jesus continues to deliver me from many yokes and bondages, including fake idols, new age ties, and much deception.

Therefore, if anyone is in Christ, the new creation has come: The old has gone, the new is here!
2 Corinthians 5:17-18 9

I continue to hear the voice of God more and more. He calls me beloved and keeps me and my children under the protection of His love.

My Heavenly Father lifted me up from terrible

hurt brought about by bondage and deception and showed me a real Father's love. Later, He also showed me the love and protection of a Divine husband.

Jesus is my best friend and spiritual husband. It is a love that cannot be found anywhere and from anyone on earth. A love so outrageous, deep, and loving that it takes my breath away…

I have found my true worth as a woman. As a precious daughter of my Father and as a bride of Christ.

As I look over the tapestry of my life, and the myriad of ways it could have gone, through all the pain and joy, I see a beautiful love story emerge with my first Love, God, the keeper of my heart and my soul.

It took me decades of searching in many wrong places and experiencing several painful moments to seek the elusive answer to the empty place in my soul. The truth. The absolute truth. Jesus is the Way, the Truth, and the Life.

Winston Churchill said that the truth is so valuable that it is attended to by a bodyguard of lies. Mark Twain said the most valuable thing we have is the truth. At four years old when my Father in Heaven came down to comfort me and guide me through many a storm, little did I know that I would have to penetrate a bodyguard of lies to find what I had been seeking for my whole life.

Do you care about the truth? The Absolute truth? I ask you with great urgency to call to Jesus while He can be found to accept Him as your Lord and Savior.

I know with divine certainty that Jesus, the powerful loving son of God, is the only way to meet my Father. I can only imagine what a glorious day it will be when I meet my secret God!

The journey thus far has been epic, and the love story continues through this book. As I continue to study the word of God and understand His ways, I am convinced that God knows the beginning and the end not only for my life, but for all of humanity. He is the truly the Master weaver and I am in continuous awe of my Father.

I fall on my knees in gratitude. I now have more peace in my soul, and the constant torment has left me. I am truly blessed more than I deserve. And it is only the beginning…

As you read through these poems, I pray you will be swept on an adventure of emotions and truths that will capture your soul.

As we navigate the treacherous waters of

today, I have found there is no other place, but the secret place and the Bible, the word of God as delivered by God Almighty that provides direction, wisdom, peace, comfort and hope for a time such as this....

"Be still, and know that I am God"
Psalm 46:10(ESV)

Save My Soul

That fateful day when I was four
Scared and lost
No sense of reality
No ability to understand
Innocence lost
What happened?

My Father
He is in pain. Who hurt him?
I ran after him as they rolled him away

Will I see him again?
Papa, Papa, Come back

My mother on the phone
Frantic

The ambulance speeds them away
I love you Papa
Where did you go?

Rocking myself on the steps
Curled in a ball
Is it my fault?
Why did he leave me alone?

Come back please
Papa, where are you?

Amidst the pain and numbness
In that moment time stood still

A sense of comfort and peace envelopes me
I hear a voice as God swoops in
"I am here to save your soul"

—⊗—

"For My thoughts are not your thoughts,
Nor are your ways My ways," says the Lord.
"For as the heavens are higher than the earth,
So are My ways higher than your ways,
And My thoughts than your thoughts."
Isaiah 55:8-9 (NKJV)

Bullied

A warm sunny day
School is done
Walking to get my bike for my journey home

Three girls call out to me
Hey!

I stop
I am excited
Do they want to be my friends?

I follow them into a classroom
The door clicks shut behind me

They push me against a wall
They shove me
They hurl insults
It feels like an eternity

What a vicious attack
They are unashamed

They finally let me go
I am broken
I sob and sob

I cry out to my God
Why me?
Years later
I finally allow Him to heal my wounds

I can see why they would attack
A child of God is who they hate
As their souls are empty and full of pain
Ready to attack again

The heart is deceitful above all things, and desperately
wicked: who can know it?
Jeremiah 17:9 (KJV)

The Storm

The winds are howling around me
The thunder is loud

I am being torn apart
The storm is all around me

My mind is in torment
The attack is great

How do I survive?
I am crying in the rain

I am on my knees
Shouting out Your name

Save me Lord
Save me from the storm

I am at Your feet
I cannot go on
I am frightened
Lightning strikes on my life

Where are You Lord?
I am begging You to shelter me
God's answers me

There is a place
A center of calm
In the eye of the storm
The world will turn
The storms will come
But stay here
Stay with Me
Where I can calm your soul

Then you will call upon Me and go
and pray to Me, and I will listen to you.
And you will seek Me and find Me
when you search for Me with all your heart.
Jeremiah 29:12-13 (NKJV)

Hope Lost

I am wearing a crown
Roses thrown at my feet
The crowd is cheering
I feel like I am floating on air

I won!
Me?
The girl from nowhere

The question asked?
Is Beauty skin deep and why?
I respond
True beauty comes from within
Within your heart and soul

Wait!

The judges are bribed
The crown is taken
Injustice!
I am broken
The girl from nowhere
Did I really matter after all?

The thief does not come except to steal,
and to kill, and to destroy.
I have come that they may have life,
and that they may have it more abundantly.
John 10:10 (NKJV)

Backstory: I was encouraged to compete in Miss India Zimbabwe and won. Forty-five minutes later after I had been crowned and the roses had been thrown at my feet, the judges reversed their decision and said that the scores had not been added up correctly. I learned that many people had seen the father of the first princess, who was a wealthy lawyer, go up to the judges. After an intense discussion, he bribed them. His daughter took my crown.

Lost in the Dark

Here I am
I am broken
I am scared

My soul is tormented
My soul is lost

The world deceived me
It hurt me
It destroyed me

I looked in all the wrong places
Damaged from the world and sin
My world is falling in
The darkness destroys my soul

Help, Help, Help me!
I cry into the wilderness
Hear my heart
Hear my cry

My soul is seeking
Who will help me?
Who will save my soul?

I seek a place of comfort
A place of peace
A place of rest for my weary soul

The world does not know me
Who will save me?
Who will love me through it all?

I kneel, O Lord, at Your feet
To save my wretched soul

Seek the Lord while he may be found.
all on him while he is near.
Isaiah 55:6

Empty Soul

What is that empty feeling
A burning in my soul
A desperate need to fill this void

Always seeking
There must be something more

Seek something, anything to calm my soul
Where do I turn?
Sex, Drugs, Alcohol?

The desire to connect
I seek my secret God instead

No matter what I do
It becomes empty and meaningless
There is still a burning in my soul

So, flee youthful passions
and pursue righteousness, faith, love, and peace,
along with those who call on the Lord
from a pure heart.
2 Timothy 2:22 (ESV)

Deception

Wake up
You are asleep

The father of lies
Deception is his game

He hides in the dark and hates the light
He plays with your mind

There is an internal struggle
Something is not quite right

You choose to believe
In a world of lies

You can pretend
But cannot hide

Your freedom is at risk
He wants you to fall

He tempts you in countless ways
He knows your weakness

You know the truth deep in your soul
Have a heart to listen
Have eyes to see
Ears to hear

Be aware

Repent and turn
Before it is too late

Do not be deceived: God cannot be mocked.
A man reaps what he sows'
Galatians 6:7-10

Journey of Life

As you journey through life
You will encounter many things
Sorrows and Joy
Pain and Victory
Choices

It is in the journey
Where you will find Me
If you look

I am always with you
When you fall
When you win
When you obey
When you sin
I share your pain
I share your joy

When you are tired and hurt
I will give you strength
When you are scared and lost
Have courage and faith
Do not be afraid
I am always with you

No matter how many times you fall
Call my name
I will pick you up

We can start together all over again

Walk with Me on your journey of life
You will never feel alone
If you seek Me
If you call My name

Finally, brethren, whatever things are true, whatever
things are noble, whatever things are just, whatever
things are pure, whatever things are lovely, whatever
things are of good report,
if there is any virtue and if there is anything
praiseworthy—meditate on these things.
Philippians 4:8 (NKJV)

Choices

I gave you free will
I gave you choice

You can choose to see the light
You can choose what is right

You can choose life or death
You can choose good or evil

You can choose sin
You can choose not to sin

You can choose to lose
You can choose to win

Choose your words
Choose your ways

Choose truth
Choose lies

The choice is yours
You have free will

Choose wisely
There is always consequence

Destruction or Life
Darkness or Light

I say Choose Life
Choose Light

The choice is yours
You have free will

You have the power to decide
So, Choose

I call heaven and earth to witness against you today,
that I have set before you life and death,
blessing and curse.
Deuteronomy 30:19a (ESV)

If you fully obey the Lord your God
and carefully follow all his commands,
I give you today,
the Lord your God will set you high
above all the nations on earth.
All these blessings will come on you
and accompany you
if you obey the Lord your God.
Deuteronomy 28:1-2

Deep Calls to Deep

Deep calls to Deep
My Father
My soul desperately calls out to You

My brokenness
hidden deep within

What did they do to me?
Why did they hurt me?

I only sought protection
I only sought love

My soul cries deep within
Broken in a thousand pieces

Yet, I carry on
Pretending that I am fine

I seek control so I can protect myself
Believing that no one can hurt me again

I learn to please others
Afraid of another attack
I sometimes hide so they do not see me

I become externally fierce and proud
Yet my soul is so weak

I am religious and critical
Somehow thinking that I am the judge and jury
Like my opinions are so righteous
So stuck and unwilling to hear that I could be
wrong

I lie to the world and I lie to myself
I walk around as
a shadow of my true self.

Deep calls to Deep

Hear my soul cry out in the wilderness
Save me Father!

The purposes of a person's heart
are deep waters,
but one who has insight draws them.
Proverbs 20:5

Do You Hear Me?

I call again. I know He exists
He is my only hope

I shout
Lord!
Do You hear me?

I am on my knees
I am begging and pleading for mercy
Do You hear me?

I am crying so hard
That my soul is being torn apart
Do You hear me my Lord?

I am in the wilderness
It is dark
I feel alone
Where are You my Lord?
I know You exist
You are my only hope

I cry
I shout out His name
Over and over again
I cannot go through this alone

As I sit on a park bench
Sobbing uncontrollably
Calling for my Lord again

He sends a homeless man
Who stops to comfort me
He tells me
As he looks up to the sky
The Lord He sent me
He heard your cries
Something speaks deep into my soul

God must have heard me
I thought

For a moment
I feel sense of hope
A glimmer that this pain will end

That God would send an angel in disguise
Who was homeless as could be
Would be the one to comfort me

I see a light
A reason to carry on
I am not alone in the wilderness
The Lord He does hear me

He does hear my cry
He will deliver me
He is my only hope

I sob at the feet of the cross
Where Jesus is slain
Lord have mercy
Can You also feel my pain?

Please save me
How much longer?

It has been a while
How much longer do I endure this pain?
The darkest hour is before the dawn
I hold onto a strand of hope
Surely, my Lord will never forsake me
He will deliver me
From the deception and bondage of the evil one

Then comes a day
I see a ray of sunshine
The clouds begin to disappear
I begin to feel renewed

My burden starts to become lighter
I hear a voice
I heard you My beloved
I held your hand and was with you through it all
I gave you strength and grace to stay the course

I felt your pain
I cried with you

My child it was for a season
But I delivered you

I can do all things through Christ
who strengthens me.
Philippians 4:13 (KJV)

Not only so, but we also glory in our sufferings,
because we know that suffering produces perseverance;
perseverance, character;
and character, hope.
Romans 5:3-4

Truth

My Truth
Your truth
The Truth

Information so easily spread
There are many voices

Who is telling the truth?
Who do we believe?

God, I ask You?
What do we do?

The truth is the truth
It will come into the light

The truth is so powerful that it is hidden
under a mountain of lies

Yes Lord
True
But who to believe?

My child
Be Still

Don't fear
Disconnect

Listen to your own quiet voice
It is God within you that directs your thoughts

Here you will find peace
The truth will then appear
The noise of the world will soon disappear

Then you will walk strong
With no fear
For I am with you
Through it all
Hear only My voice
The truth will set you free

Then you will know the truth,
and the truth will set you free."
John 8:32

Gods Relentless Love

A wretched soul like me
Lost and unholy

Confused and carnal
Living in a world of sin

Thinking I am right
Thinking I am in control

How lofty I am
So full of pride

I get thrown to the wolves
I still resist

Thinking somehow, I can save myself
By myself

The world pulls me in all directions
I am tormented and know something is missing
Deep in my soul

Then one day I am stopped by a stranger
Maybe an angel in disguise?

And he tells me
God has been watching me
Jesus can save you

I mock him
I can do this by myself

It takes some years before I concede
So, lost and broken and deceived

When another stranger
Maybe an angel in disguise?

Tells me that Jesus can save me
I fall on my knees

Tell me how
I am ready to listen

No, in all these things we are more than conquerors
through him who loved us.
For I am convinced that neither death nor life,
neither angels nor demons, neither the present nor the
future, nor any powers, neither height nor depth,
nor anything else in all creation,
will be able to separate us from the love of God
that is in Christ Jesus our Lord.
Romans 8:37-39

Trapped

My life like a bird trapped in a dark cage
No idea of how to be free

Hard to breathe. Cannot move.
Stuck
Surviving in the only world I know

God whispers in my ear
Fly little bird the door is open.
You can be free

I look out for a moment.
My heart leaps as it envisions
a future that could be

But I am scared to leave as the cage comforts me
It is the only world I know.

I resist.
God persists.

Years of whispers. Tempted by the open door.
I escape the cage for moments,
only to be attacked once more.

Back to the cage the place that comforts me
Stuck not free, but the only world I know.

Gods voice calls louder and says
little bird be free
How God how? Please stay with me.

It is all an illusion. You are deceived.
My mind transforms and now I see

I trapped myself
Fly bird fly be free.

I leave the cage. My life expands.
I can breathe and I am free.

God whispers in my ear
be the eagle you were meant to be
Possibilities are endless.

A sense of power runs through me.
I soar into the sky and the world discovers the true
me.
I once was trapped and now I am free

But they who wait for the Lord
shall renew their strength;
they shall mount up with wings like eagles;
they shall run and not be weary;
they shall walk and not faint.
Isaiah 40:31 (ESV)

Meeting Jesus

An idol worshipper
A lost soul
I mocked
How can you say the only way is through the son?

Who is Jesus?
Asking my God
Is He really the way, truth, and life?
I trust You only my God
Show me if this is true

I embark on a journey of discovery
So interesting that the Bible predicted
over thousands of years before
the exact place Jesus would be born.
Prophecy foretold and Prophecy realized
History unfolds before my eyes
My Bible knowledge has increased
Christians appearing out the blue
Telling me that the word is true

Months and months of searching
Now distraught
Still not believing
God please tell me
No one else
Only You I trust
Standing in a circle
Praying for the first time with believers

Looking up in desperation asking my Lord
Tell me please I have waited for so long

In that moment
I am pushed backwards
By a force that I do not know

I am speaking words that I do not understand
There is excitement
A visitor is in our space
I look up and see Jesus' face
Jesus is the Way, Truth, and Life!
The God of the Universe
He told me Himself.

Jesus answered,
"I am the way and the truth and the life.
No one comes to the Father except through me."
John 14:6

Time Stands Still

Time stands still
As I stare into His face

Falling, falling into His sapphire eyes
Deeper than the ocean
More beautiful than anything I have ever seen

His eyes full of light
Limitless
Powerful
Divine

As He stares back at me
I am mesmerized by my King
Enveloped by His love
I am undone

Where have You been Jesus all my life?
I am at a point of no return

In that moment
Time stands still
Falling, Falling into His sapphire eyes

But blessed are your eyes because they see,
and your ears because they hear.
Matthew 13:16

There was Jesus presented as a King!
In that moment of meeting Him
I was mesmerized and captivated by my Lord.
It felt like time had stood still
and I had entered another world

Climb with Me

You now are saved
You now walk with Christ
You are on a new journey and it has just begun

Let us climb together, child
Hold My hand, child, as we climb higher and
higher to see mightier and miraculous things

To get to the top
To enjoy the journey
To see the miracles
To expand your gifts

There are things that you must give up
The ways and habits of your old life
As you are a new creation
Born again to see a new life

As you climb and release the baggage of sin,
I will be with you
The enemy will try to make you fall
Fall back to the bottom of the mountain if he can
The enemy will seduce you to go back to your old
self
It seems easier to just give up

Don't!

Climb with strength up the mountain
You are courageous and strong
Climb with the word of God!

As you seek Me
As you read My word
Your spirit will get lighter
You will climb faster
You will hear My voice more and more

I will guide you
I will help you
Call to Me My child

I call to you my Lord
I read Your word
The storms begin to disappear
There is a peace that I have never felt before

Rest a while with Me My child
Bask in My presence
Get filled with the Spirit
You will get stronger and stronger
Nothing can stop you from reaching the top
You are now climbing with the God Almighty

I stay close to Him
Our journey is glorious and full of adventure

Miracles start to happen
My gifts expand
Blessings chase me up the mountain
Lord, Lord, Lord

I am grateful
I am blessed
I am fulfilled
I am full of the Holy Spirit
I am full of peace

In You my God I trust
I have arrived
You have been there at every step and every fall

I bask and delight in Your divine presence
Day and night

As we sit and watch the sunrise and sunset
From the highest peak
We contemplate
What a journey it has been
The journey was worth more than gold
You share with me the essence of Your soul

What love You have for me, my Lord
To stay with me through it all

The earth is the Lord's, and everything in it,
the world, and all who live in it;
for he founded it on the seas
and established it on the waters.
Who may ascend the mountain of the Lord?
Who may stand in his holy place?
The one who has clean hands and a pure heart,
who does not trust in an idol
or swear by a false god.
They will receive blessing from the Lord
and vindication from God their Savior.
Such is the generation of those who seek him,
who seek your face, God of Jacob.
Psalm 24: 1-6

The Lighthouse

I yearn to spend time with You, Oh Lord
As You yearn to spend time with me
I gravitate towards the light
The darkness pulls me back

I get distracted
Life takes over
So much to do

God asks child,
where are you?
Come spend time with Me

My heart aches and knows something is missing.
An emptiness inside.
Trying to fill the void to avoid spending time with
God

I get thrown to and fro by the waves of emotion
I need You Father
What stops me? I know it is the best place to be

I finally sit in solitude feeling a peace that quiets
my soul
The beautiful silence and love that flows through
me.

Then I remember to move towards the light

And sit quietly with God
My soul quietens as God comforts me with His
presence

My God. My Lighthouse.
In the stormy sea of life
The only place to be.

Again, Jesus spoke to them, saying,
"I am the light of the world.
Whoever follows me will not walk in darkness
but will have the light of life."
John 8:12 (ESV)

God Remember Me

God Remember Me
My heart calls out
To become whom, I was meant to be

There is a disconnect
Two worlds that collide
Who I am now and who You created me to be
There is more to discover than what I see

Hear my voice
Hear my cries
Where are You Lord?
Please remember me

You do not forget who You created me to be
Reveal Your purpose
Remove the veils
Please let me see

God Remember me
To become whom, I was meant to be

Do not remember the sins of my youth
and my rebellious ways;
according to your love remember me,
for you, Lord, are good.
Psalm 25:7

Wrestling with God

I will no longer wrestle with You, Oh Lord
I will no longer stand in Your way
I wanted to do it my way
I wanted to be in control

I surrender
I allow You to guide my path
I am open to Your voice and wisdom
I am no longer a willful obstacle in Your way

You know the beginning from the end
I don't
You know what's better for me than I do
I don't
I surrender

I have tried it my way
It's exhausting
It's painful

I submit my life to You, Oh Lord
I surrender

Keep me in all Your ways
Protect me and my family, Oh Lord

I now walk with You instead of against You.
I surrender

Submit yourselves therefore to God.
Resist the devil, and he will flee from you.
James 4:7

Faith of a Mustard Seed

All it takes is one step
Just one

One step that takes you into the light
One step away from the darkness
Just one

I hear the voice of God
Have faith

Faith My child
Just take one step with Me
Do not let the darkness pull you back

I take the step
Just one
Just one into the light
I do not let the darkness pull me back

I call out
Holy Spirt please lead me
Lord Jesus help me!

My faith like a fragile flower
Coming up for the first time from underground
Seeking sunshine
Seeking light

Please do not let the darkness
Trample over me

I took one step
my Lord
Just one

I can do this
A seed was planted a long time ago
My Faith starts to grow
I start to flourish
Watered by the word of God
In His presence
My worries melt away

I am filled with peace
A joy
A certainty
That I am not alone

I walk with faith when I am right on the edge
When I am about to fall
That is when I know to call
Father
I trust You
I will take one step
Just one

It never fails
He never fails
He pulls me back

He saves me again and again
And again

My Father
A seed was planted a long time ago
My Faith has grown

I am so grateful for Your love and mercy
Thank You for the blessings
Yes, even miracles!
Thank You for saving me

It took that one step
Just one

I had no idea
How incredible the journey would be
And that one day I would grow into a mighty oak
tree

He said to them, "Because of your little faith.
For truly, I say to you,
if you have faith like a grain of mustard seed,
you will say to this mountain,
'Move from here to there,' and it will move,
and nothing will be impossible for you."
Matthew 17:20 (ESV)

A Searching God

I searched far and wide
I looked for you all over the earth

I climbed on top of mountains
Swam across the seas
Searching for you

Searching for that one moment
That moment I could say

I have found a precious soul
That would know My name

How I looked and looked
So, I could tell you

That you are so beloved
How much you mean to Me

That you would hear Me whisper
That you always belonged to Me

Your Father who Art in Heaven
A Father who will never give up on you
A Father who knows your name
A Father who loves you through time and eternity

I love those who love me,
and those who seek me diligently find me.
Proverbs 8:17 (NKJV)

Beloved

My dear daughter
How long I have waited for you

I love you My daughter
As the depths of the ocean and the highest
mountains

You are beloved
You are My child that I held in the bosom of My
heart

You are bold and kind
A blessing to mankind

The light is bright
Do not be afraid
Call to Me
And I will hear

I will answer your prayers
The blessings of Jabez is upon you

Start to see the bright light
Bold and Beautiful in the night

The sky will light up for the world to see
Who I created you to be

You have no idea how brightly your light shines
A time of new beginnings for blessings and joy

A time of preparation
For a time for such as this
My dear daughter
How long I have waited for you

Where has your beloved gone,
O most beautiful among women?
Where has your beloved turned,
That we may seek him with you?
Song of Solomon 6:1 (ESV)

God's Deep Love

I created you in the womb
I know who you are
You are beautiful and kind
A blessing to mankind

I loved you from the beginning and I will love you
to the end
You are in My heart for all eternity

I love you deeply and completely
To give you hope and serenity

Stay close to Me as I stay close to you

Pray and never give up on Me
I will never give up on you
I am always here, hold My hand as we grow
together
Now and through eternity

I praise you,
for I am fearfully and wonderfully made.
Wonderful are your works; my soul knows it very well.
Psalm 139:14 (ESV)

Blessed Gifts

See my children, O Lord
See how beautiful they are

See the beauty and the wonder of their souls
Your precious gifts to me to hold

I see the light that shines through them
A chance to guide their souls

How much You must love them
How much You must love me

Bless their souls
Protect their hearts

May they follow You
My Lord
In all their ways

Surround them with Your love
Protect them in every way

Thank You for my blessings
My Children, My Life
For sharing their hearts of gold

I am so grateful
My soul overflows

But Jesus said,
"Let the little children come to me
and do not hinder them,
for to such belongs the kingdom of heaven."
Matthew 19:14 (ESV)

Precious Child

My dear child from before
You are so precious to me

When you were born
The angels were delighted by the vision they saw

The sky was silent and asleep
When you woke up my little one
You opened your eyes and the sky lit up

Your eyes were so bright
The dark sky was bedazzled with light

You shone like the sun
So beautiful to behold

I stood back at my creation
Filled with tears of joy

Your heart and soul, such perfection
There is no other as beautiful as you

As I held you by my beating heart
Know this
I love you more than you could ever know

She is more precious than jewels,
and nothing you desire can compare with her.
Proverbs 3:15 ESV

Behold, children are a heritage from the Lord,
the fruit of the womb a reward.
Psalm 127:3 ESV

The Touch of God

Touched by the hand of God
There is no turning back

My eyes are opened
An adventure begins
My soul transforms

I will follow You
To the ends of the earth
And from Beersheba to Galilee

You are mighty
You are kind
You renew my mind

Blessings Abound!
You set me upon high

God You are so good
You are so wise

A touch of God is all it takes
To transform my life

I am forever indebted
My Father, My Lord
For Your divine touch of my soul.

Anyone who does not love does not know God,
because God is love.
Matthew 22:37 (NKJV)

The touch of God in the heart is so precious, as it is so deep and intimate and personal. God pierces through all our layers and touches the core of our being. This is the secret place where we are deeply known and loved for who we are and whose we are.

My Love for God

God how much do You bear
How much do You cry?
God how much do You care
About our wretched souls

Who cries for You?
Who comforts You?
When Your creation goes astray
I love You God
You are my savior
You are my friend
I love You more each day

I hope You feel my love
As I feel Yours
Thank You, Lord, for all You do
I love You more than I can say

For God so loved the world,
that he gave his only Son,
that whoever believes in him should not perish
but have eternal life.
John 3:16

Who Are You My God?

You are an enigma
A mystery
I try to find words
To describe You

You seem so far
Yet You are so close

So surreal
But so real

You are everywhere
In the trees.
In the seas
In my heart
In the depths of my soul

I hear You in my son's laughter
I see You in my daughter's eyes

I look in the mirror
I see You looking back at me
Telling me that You created me
Telling me that I am fearfully and wonderfully
made

I feel Your presence when I look at Your creation
The winding rivers
The splendor of a sunset
The majestic mountain ranges
The beauty of a smile

You are so smart
So wise
You are so merciful
So Faithful
So, loving and kind

You are above all
My Father
My Lord
My Savior
The essence of my soul

Jesus said to him,
"You shall love the LORD your God with all your heart,
with all your soul, and with all your mind."
John 4:8 (NKJV)

God's Creation

I want fly into the sky
On angels' wings
Free and powerful
Seeing the world below

The beauty of Your creation
The winding rivers and the seas
The mountains and the hills
The flowers and the trees
The birds and the bees

Animals that run across the desert
Swim across the ocean
Play in the sand
Frolic in the snow

A perfect canvas
Man and woman
Your beloved creation

The uniqueness of Your mind
Your thoughts are so high
So creative, so loving and kind
As You look upon mankind

It all belongs to You
You know the Beginning from the End

The Alpha and Omega
The Creator
The Artist
The God of all Creation

You are worthy, O Lord,
To receive glory and honor and power.
For You created all things,
And by Your will they exist and were created.
Revelation 4:11 (NKJV)

Awaken

My people are asleep
They have forgotten where they came from

Looking for meaning
Looking for purpose

They are lost

Seeking idols
Seeking gold
Seeking lust

Not knowing where to turn

Deceived
Thinking that the Lord does not exist

Doing whatever they want
Not realizing they cause their own destruction

You will reap what you sow
It is a law
You cannot escape
You have been warned

Awaken My children
Awaken your spirit

Turn from Pride
Before it is too late

For God will bring every work into judgment,
Including every secret thing,
Whether good or evil.
Ecclesiastes 12:14 (NKJV)

Be sober, be vigilant;
because your adversary the devil walks about
like a roaring lion, seeking whom he may devour.
Resist him, steadfast in the faith,
knowing that the same sufferings are experienced
by your brotherhood in the world.
1 Peter 5:8-9 (NKJV)

Pride

Turn from pride
It will not serve you in the end

Open your eyes
You are deceived
The Father fights to protect His children
The child rebels

For how long?
Till you fall to the bottom of the pit?

How is it working out for you?
Do you have peace in your heart?

Seek the truth
Willful rebellion is no excuse

The constant need to be right
Not to do right

Holding steadfast to your pride
Not willing to give Me even a moment
Not willing to listen for the truth

What has you hold on so tight?
Fear?
Are you even willing to listen?

Seek truth
How many times do you want to fall?
Before you turn from pride

For the sin of their mouth and the words of their lips
Let them even be taken in their pride,
And for the cursing and lying which, they speak.
Psalm 59:12 (NKJV)

Twisted Reality

Twisted Reality
Trapped in a perception that does not belong to
you

Your world revolves around anyone's opinion but
your own
Fearful to be your true self

Best to be quiet and hidden.
Please everyone
Not honoring who God created you to be

There is no true you
Your existence a lie

Not thinking what is right
Not wanting to see the light.

Confusion and deception
Fearful to be your true self

Come out of the shadows
Come into the light

Pray to God to reveal your birthright

Ask God Almighty to remove the veil
Reveal who are created to be

Go forth with courage and faith
Discover who you are

Allow God to guide your way
As He helps you see the power
and beauty of your true self

Expand your vision
Follow your heart

Step out to into a new world
Accept your destiny

And one day you will learn to see yourself
as God sees you
No longer deceived by a twisted reality

We know that we are children of God,
and that the whole world
is under the control of the evil one.
1 John 5:19

Gods Heart

A Mother's unconditional love for her child
Is Like God's heart

It is like how God loves you
He will do anything for you

He sees that you are perfect in His eyes
He will fight for you
He will love you more than you even understand

He stays up all night
To make sure you come safely home

He cannot ever stop loving you
No matter what you do

He yearns to spend time with you
To fill you with His love
To guide you
To give you wisdom
To provide for your every need

He wants the best for you
To see you succeed
To have a blessed life
To have peace in your soul
He is part of you as you are part of Him

He never gives up on you
You are so precious in His eyes
It is His unconditional love that will save you
That you can rely on
That will give you strength
That will carry you through this life

Let Him love you
Fall into His arms
To find rest and comfort
As He restores your soul

———❧———

Love is patient and kind;
love does not envy or boast;
it is not arrogant or rude.
It does not insist on its own way;
it is not irritable or resentful.
it does not rejoice at wrongdoing
but rejoices with the truth.
Love bears all things, believes all things,
hopes all things, endures all things.
Love never ends.
As for prophecies, they will pass away;
as for tongues, they will cease;
as for knowledge, it will pass away.
1 Corinthians 13:4-8 (ESV)

Restore My Soul

Restore my soul O Lord
Back to how You created me to be

I have been in the wilderness for so long
My soul is broken in more places than I even
know
I want so desperately to be fully healed

My soul like a patchwork quilt
Sewn together by my thoughts, desires, and
feelings
By other people's thoughts, desires, and feelings
Utter confusion

My soul fragmented in patches
From sin and pain
From deception and unbelief

In those moments I remembered to call out to You
You did comfort me,
And a piece of my soul was restored

I searched for You in many places
However, there was no need
You were always with me in my heart
You were always loving me through the pain

I did not consider until now
I should have come to You first

I did not consider Your thoughts desires and
feelings
My Father who desperately loves His child
My Father who only wants the best for me
My Father who wants to fully restore my soul

As I listen to my Father and repent at His feet
Other voices in my head are quietened

My voice
The voice of those around me
Those who I love
Even the voice of the father of lies

Confusion begins to disappear
I am now a work in progress
Listening to my Father
My Lord

I now listen to His thoughts and desires
To consider His feelings and not just my own

To believe that my Lord is truly enough
And no one else has the power to save me
My Lord has the power to heal my broken places
The power to restore my soul
Back to how to He created me to be

A multi-colored patchwork quilt
Full of light, love, and joy
So Beautiful
Sewn by the Almighty hand of God.

The Lord is my shepherd;
I shall not want.
He maketh me to lie down in green pastures:
he leadeth me beside the still waters.
He restoreth my soul: he leadeth me
in the paths of righteousness for his name's sake.
Yea, though I walk through the valley
of the shadow of death,
I will fear no evil: for thou art with me;
thy rod and thy staff they comfort me.
Thou preparest a table before me
in the presence of mine enemies:
thou anointest my head with oil;
my cup runneth over.
Surely goodness and mercy shall follow me
all the days of my life:
and I will dwell in the house of the Lord forever.
Psalm 23:1-6 (KJV)

Heaven's Door

I knock on heaven's door
My Father who art in Heaven
Please may I enter, I ask in Jesus name
To sit at Your feet
To spend a moment with You

The door of heaven
Exquisite, ingrained wood
So beautiful and majestic
Handles made of gold

My Father
He commands that the door be open

Come in My child
What a delightful surprise

I love to spend time with you
Talk to Me

I am here to help you
Here to soothe your pain
Here to give you favor
Here to love your soul

As I pour out my heart to the Lord
He gently reaches out His hand
To touch my fragile soul

I feel a love that I have never known before
surge through my entire being

I am filled with a mighty light
My soul fragile no more
As Gods love soars through me
I feel like a new creation

The Lord God Almighty
He heals me
He comforts me

He fills me with love
Just a moment to sit with Him

To honor Him
To love Him back

He tells me
Child

Just knock
And I will answer
Just ask
I will respond
I know the great things I have for you

I will listen to you
Please obey My will
Know that I will not harm you
Know that I want the best for you
Know that I am your Father
No good thing will I behold

Come humbly in My Son's name
All I ask is for you to knock on Heavens door

Ask, and it will be given to you;
seek, and you will find;
knock, and it will be opened to you.
For everyone who asks receives,
and he who seeks finds,
and to him who knocks it will be opened.
Matthew 7:7-8

Crossing the River Jordan

I did not know You Jesus
I did not know that it was You I was seeking my
whole life

Even after I finally found You
The enemy fought me relentlessly
On the other side of the river Jordan
Not wanting me to get to the promised land

I knew that there was something I needed on the
other side
I began to cross
The river was dry
I am thirsty
My knees are bleeding as I crawl across the jagged
rocks

It did not matter
I heard a gentle voice that did not stop
Calling, calling me to cross the River Jordan

Suddenly, the river flooded
I began to drown

The crocodiles they sought after me
To devour my flesh

I was taken to the bottom of the river
I was so scared
Is this my end?

I heard His voice calling to me
I cannot not give up I said

I used a strength that I knew was not all mine
To pull myself and swim back to the top
For a moment to get some air

I got pulled down again
And encountered a dark tunnel
There was no light
I had to press through with all my might
The voice would not stop calling me
Come to the other side

I could not see
I was so tired
It did not matter
I just knew I had to still forge on
I had to get to the other side

Utter exhaustion took over me
I was thirsty as could be

Seeking, seeking
Pressing, pressing
Surely, the darkness has to disappear
There must be a light at the other end

The voice it calls me
I cannot stop

I push
I fight
With all my might
I must, I must get to the other side

Battered and bruised
Hungry and Thirsty

It feels like it is taking an eternity
I suddenly see a glimmer of light
Can it be?
Can it be the end?
Can I finally get to the other side?

I am filled with hope
I press through the dark tunnel

To swim into the most beautiful clear water
I have ever seen

I am pushed by a gentle wave
To the banks of the river
Exhausted

I crossed
I crossed the River Jordan
I got to the other side!

I see a glorious sight
A beautiful man behind the voice
He was waiting for me
As I fall into His arms

He gives me healing water
He satisfies my hunger

I did not know it was You Jesus
I did not know that it was You I was seeking my
whole life

As I now surrender to You completely
To willingly follow Your every step for eternity
In the promised land.

Little children,
you are from God and have overcome them,
for he who is in you
is greater than he who is in the world.
1 John 4:4 (ESV)

Healing Waters

Do not fret My children
My righteous ones
There is light ahead

Be faithful and true
See the sky and the birds
The beautiful world
I created for you

I am GOD the Alpha and Omega
I am in control

Do not worry
Do not be afraid

Sing and be happy
Dance with joy!

The Healing water is going to flow
through the Land

Then the angel showed me the river
of the water of life, bright as crystal,
flowing from the throne of God
and of the Lamb
through the middle of the street of the city;
also, on either side of the river,
the tree of life with its twelve kinds of fruit,
yielding its fruit each month.
The leaves of the tree
were for the healing of the nations.
Revelation 22:1-2 (ESV)

Whoever believes in me,
as the Scripture has said,
"Out of his heart will flow rivers of living water."
John 7:38 (ESV)

When you pass through the waters,
I will be with you;
and through the rivers,
they shall not overwhelm you;
when you walk through fire you shall not be burned,
and the flame shall not consume you.
Isaiah 43:2 (ESV)

Victory

Holy Spirit You are so gentle in Your ways
You showed me the error of my ways

The parts of me that are healed cannot be shaken
Jesus's love has mended the broken places

Delivered from torment
Deep pain has disappeared
Scars are fading

As I sit still
And listen to Gods voice
His love and kindness fill my soul

Destiny starts to fall into place
My soul rejoices and feels empty no more

The Kingdom of Light
Has claimed me for eternity

Victory is the Lords!
Victory is mine.

He heals the brokenhearted
and binds up their wounds.
Psalm 147:3

For every child of God defeats this evil world,
and we achieve this victory through our faith.
1 John 5:4

Esther

Yellow rose petals are thrown on the courtroom
floor

Here comes Esther
Holding a glorious scepter

Dressed in white and gold
So beautiful to behold

Her eyes they shine as bright as the stars
Her face aglow with Gods glory

She walks with Grace and Dignity
Her heart shows no Iniquity

She is the daughter of the most High God
She is the chosen queen

To serve her King and her people
My beloved, Queen Esther!

For if you remain silent at this time,
relief and deliverance for the Jews
will arise from another place,
but you and your father's family will perish.
And who knows but that you have come
to your royal position for such a time as this?
Esther 4:14

Salvation Prayer

The salvation prayer changes a person's eternal destiny.

The Bible says praying to receive Christ is as easy as asking. Of course, one must ask in faith.

It is important to hear the Gospel because God draws people to His Son through the truth.

No one can come to me
unless the Father who sent me draws him.
And I will raise him up on the last day.
It is written in the Prophets,
'And they will all be taught by God.'
Everyone who has heard
and learned from the Father comes to me.
John 6:44-45

Lord Jesus,

I now confess to You all the wrong and sinful things that I have ever done in my life. I ask that You please forgive me and wash away all my sins by the blood that You have personally shed for me on the cross.

I believe that Jesus Christ came as the Son of Man and the Son of God, then rose from the dead on the third day to give all of us eternal life. I am now ready to accept You as my personal Lord and Savior, I now ask that You come into my life and live with me for all of eternity.

Father, Jesus – I now believe that I am truly saved and born again.

Thank You Father. Thank You Jesus.

For Everyone who calls on the name of the Lord
shall be saved.
But how are they to call on one
in whom they have not believed?
And how are they to believe in one
of whom they have never heard?
And how are they to hear
without someone to proclaim him?
And how are they to proclaim him unless they are sent?
As it is written, "How beautiful are the feet of those
who bring good news!"
But not all have obeyed the good news;
for Isaiah says, "Lord, who has believed our message?"
So, faith comes from what is heard,
and what is heard comes through the word of Christ.
Romans10:13-17 (NRSV)

About the Author

Trupti Desai was born in Zimbabwe to immigrant parents from Gujarat, India. Trupti has traveled all over the world to witness the wonders of God She currently lives in Texas with her family and is a devoted mother to her three wonderful children.

Trupti always had a strong relationship with God and has a recollection of hearing His voice at the age of four. She has a beautiful gift to be able to go behind the veil and connect with the heart of God. Trupti was brought up in the Hindu religion and was powerfully saved in 2016 when she began her journey with Jesus.

Contact Information
EsthersSoul@gmail.com